PJ NTSOANE
P.O. Box 941, Lebowakgomo 0737
+2771 505 2333
POLOKWANE, LIMPOPO PROVINCE, RSA

First Published in 2014

ISBN: 978-0-9922330-3-7

Cover design and illustrations by Marcus Ntsoane

Foreword

This poetry book by Mungoni Manoge tackles all spheres of human life through its vivid imagery. He uses understandable easy to understand figurative language which appeals to all human senses making it enjoyable to read. You cannot have enough of it.

Contents

1. Africans

We are united by common umbilical cord,
That is the miracle of our Heavenly Lord.
We have common origin;
In the roots of Africa when she was a virgin;
When the rivers were flowing with milk and honey,
That is when we had not tasted the evil of money.
The riches of our colourful soil,
were still lying in their natural coil.

Now the birds of Africa only sing a sad song;
The melancholy lyrics of the song are too strong,
They pierce the senses of a man's spirit.
The African spirit is now split;
Egoism has become a pandemic affliction,
Fraternity and altruism face total attrition.
Instead of covering,
We are stabbing each other in the back.
We nurture this blue blabbering,
Empty shells say darkness denotes being black.

African children are trapped out there somewhere;
Alienation is forever in their glare;
They long to bask in the African Sun,
That is where their progeny will wallow in fun.
They desire to breathe in fresh African air,
That will be the only time to say: 'Life is fair.'

2. No Money this Month

We the kids see our father coming home,
We bustle barefoot to meet him.
Our tiny hands give him a warm welcome,
Daddy, we haven't seen him for months.
Like a bird feeding its nestlings,
He drops toffees into our mouths.

Like a gentle giant he hurls us up,
With a bright moon smile he gives us a head rub,
He says, "You have grown up fast."
Then he turns and stands like a mast;
His eyes are fixed on Mom,
She is giving him a storm.

She has opened her hands to receive,
Daddy is saying something we don't perceive.
I see Mommy look down,
With a quiver she points to the town,
That is where Daddy works.
Robbers even took his perks;
No money this month, that's why,
"Mommy, please don't cry."

3. My Sweet

I have never met you eye to eye;
It is so slippery to grasp the reason why,
I am filled with you.
Your beauty is like a wireless remote,
You make me do the things that I do.

I always dream about your diamond eyes,
They grip my imagination like a vice.
You are my sweet fantasy,
No wonder I ponder in sweet ecstasy.

You live somewhere I can't physically come,
Only my imagination finds your home.
I carry your picture in my pocket,
Ogling at it I never forget.

I hope one day you will know,
So that there will be no more cover to blow.
I will only breathe a marathon sigh of relief,
when I get rid of this boulder of a grief.

4. The Death of Truth

My idol made me swallow my praises of him,
The revered saint shamed me with his wicked whim.
My celebrated moral preacher;
He took a U-turn to become an immoral cheater.

The bitter truth is that sweet truth has died;
Her siblings and disciples have cried,
Detectives failed to unmask this murder mystery,
Those strong ones have abruptly become jelly-jittery.

The mourning and burial in the morning,
The sad passing was without a warning.
Just like a thief it swept through the night,
All and sundry were only surprised at daylight.

Then they wished they had the eyes of an owl,
So they could attest to the foul brawl.

5. Man's Survival

Lord did you make your children unequal?
To the lucky few the grasp of riches is a ritual;
While many others only have a pipe dream,
Only a few are entitled to the cream.

Majority only know the pangs of hunger,
Life in the ghetto is forever in danger;
There are criminals, mice and lice.
Politicians can still afford to tell camera lies;
Their purses can purchase fabricated truth,
And a dose of anaesthetic to remove a rotten tooth

We have empty promises that they will build a house;
All we have is one more guest mouse,
It comes in through the gaping cracks,
And it ravages our shabby shacks.

6. The Holes Are Full

The holes are full for glassy hypocrites,
They perform their cleansing rites.
They have forgotten to learn how to swim;
Now that the holes are flooded to the brim;
They scurry like scared rats,
They wish for the wings of bats.

The economies are plunging,

The big dogs are busy munching,
The little puppies look on and wail.
They try hard to wag the tail,
No iota of strength is left.
Families are bereft,
The inflation is running high,
It is felt by the man with a tie,
It hits hard the man in the street,
Like thorns it pricks those with bare feet.
People are asking questions,
And there are no answers as per instructions.

Some people somewhere sneeze,
Down here we feel the squeeze,
Our feeble currency catches a cold.
Somebody has to be bold,
And look the beast in the eye,
Chain it, condition it and let it die.

7. Hush My Little Sister

Hush, my little sister don't worry,
Even though our home seems awry,
This coming Easter we shall be merry.
Our mouths shall taste sweet berry,
Mom is coming home soon.
She will fill up our wooden spoon,
And we shall no longer be alone,
She has long been gone.

During biting winter-chill weather;

Like lost lambs we used to cuddle together;
With tear droplets in your eyes,
Your hand grip was as tight as vice.
You would ask for Mom's whereabouts;
When wolves outside were roaring aloud,
I reassured your little heart.
Our lives were rock-hard,
Like a knight in shining armour,
Mother will make our home warmer.

8. My Partner

I expose my closet to you,
You show the enemy our weakest crew.
In their blitz you see a flying disc,
Like the weakest link you put us at risk.

Word gets a pass,
The whole enemy world is on us.
When things get amiss,
Thunderstorms ruining our bliss,
You begin to wonder why.
When the wings can't make us fly,
You begin to think it is a curse,
Things are not getting better but worse.

Now it is time to stop and think,
Thanks to you, we are now on the parting brink.

9. Where is Noah?

Everywhere I turn my eyes,
I see floods on the rise.
We are struggling to fight the waters,
Children want to know the crux of matters.

Everywhere safe havens are flooding,
Problems keep on budding.
Health hazards multiply like mushroom,
Mother Earth is facing looming doom.
Where is Noah with his ark?
The scenery looks stark.

Threats of wars shriek in our ears,
The priests fall flat trying to allay our fears.
There are rumours of wars of mass destruction,
Nations brandish weapons of attrition.

The poor are pushed into the wasteland,
They have to rake up a living in the desert sand,
Their cries fade out in the lifeless wilderness,
The rich's billions still can't buy them happiness.

10. We Wonder Why

We watch other nations prosper,
Our very own begins to totter,
It's like a house on a sandy foundation.
We easily fall to enemy occupation,
Then we wonder why.

We see other people laughing,
When as cats and dogs we are forever fighting.
Crime rate has rocketed sky high,
It is fanned by the waves of agony cry.
Our blood is boiling with vengeance;
Peace is never given a chance,
Still we wonder why.

We have become bigheaded;
Our handshakes are heavily leaded;
Like dominoes we are bound to fall,
Unless we stand up and walk tall,
Let's take giant steps to build this country.

11. Welcome To My Shack

This is the zigzagging track,
That leads us up to my humble shack.
Welcome home Missy,
Life has never been easy.

It is nothing like your father's mansion;
But here you will get real passion;
It is sweeter than stalk toffee,
The aroma is more tantalizing than coffee.

Come and sit on my simple chair.
Let me give you the best tender care,
Here in my simple place of abode,
Please, feel free to offload.

I am chiseled for your comfort,
The sweetness you can always afford.

12. The Fraudster

You potbellied old ogre,
You embezzle your luxury from many an oke.
You abuse your usurped might to incite fright;
You sow weeds among peace crops at night;
You shun light like an owl,
The innocent like dogs they crawl,
To their submissiveness you pop champagne,
Your prosperity is reaped in the poor's pain.

You embellish your allegations with lies;
You embed the innocent with cries.
Yesterday your allies embroiled in a fist fight,
You couldn't supply them with embrocation,
Despite being the one who embattled them.
Your victim is always cut like a succulent stem;
It eludes me why some embrace your lordship,
It beats me why they keep their worship.

Deluded forces uphold your wicked emblem,
The righteous will embark on a toppling problem.
It's tantalizing to see your head spin,
When you succumb to a kick to the chin,
You are a shame indeed.

13. The Broken Pieces

I couldn't believe my eyes;
My whole body felt as cold as ice;
This life I lived for a million years,
Before my tearful eyes it disappears.
The splinter pieces are hard to retrieve,
This is not how I was led to believe.
My hope is now broken pieces,
Dry are those erstwhile warm kisses.

A strange name your heart bears,
Your caresses that stranger now wears,
The best seamstress failed with her stitches,
Instead we reaped multiple hitches.

This was the test we hopelessly failed,
Let the divorce documents be mailed.

14. The Son of Mine Worker

I am the son of a mine worker;
I am an expert long distance walker;
I walk thousands of miles to school,
My Dad says education is a freedom tool.
He earns measly wages,
He hasn't consumed many pages.

He takes a lift to the oven of the earth,
Where he is forever daring death,
He is like a bare-hand lion fighter.

His future isn't any brighter,
There is no light at the end of the tunnel,
Many of his comrades slip through a death funnel.

Rocks are falling on them like hail,
A house wife back home can only wail.
Her heavy numb hands are carried on her head,
Life has suddenly become as heavy as lead.
Doom and gloom cover the horizon,
Poverty has become her eternal prison.
They churned out a zillion,
But were chucked out like chaff.

Lord, save my Daddy,
Let him into Heaven when he is old and ready.
Make him see his great-grandchildren;
Allow him to play with them often,
When he dies with smiles they'll surround his coffin.

15. The Generation Gap

Parents and their children are heavily panting,
Mutual understanding is found wanting.
Parents, give the youth gradual freedom,
That will generate independent wisdom.

So let's close the generation gap;
Don't give the youth your old cap;
Neither must they inherit your weak heart,
They deserve a firm foundation for a start.

Their bright future is at stake,
They have to be kept awake.
They shouldn't stumble and fall,
Their ears should hear the justice call.

They don't need wax-clogged ears,
Wipe away their burning tears.

16. New Born Baby

You newborn baby look so innocent,
You descended from Heavens so decent.
You will be given a brand new name,
The world will not be the same.
This name is only a human tag,
We hope you will not be a drag.
You are a newcomer to the earth,
The world is elated at your birth.

Tomorrow you will know the wilderness,
Sometimes you will be deprived of happiness.
You will breathe in God-made fresh air;
You will cope with man-made polluted air,
They will tell you to beautify your hair.

You will know about nuking nuclear energy;
You'll deal with the oppressor's strategy;
Your bowl will sometimes be filled with delusion,
Eat with selection to evade pollution.
You will board planes with myriad minds,
You'll fulfill missions and agendas of all kinds.

You'll sometimes lose your grip;
Then you will eat by a drip,
When that time comes don't despair.
You will meet someone to make a pair;
You will know tribal and racial prejudice;
You need to throw in your witty dice,
Often open your eyes wide,
Let the wicked have no place to hide.

17. The Hooligan

Uneasy night is coming,
The whole neighbourhood is shivering.
It is the return of the reign of the hooligan,
The heartless ruffian is doting on a gun.

Some are wielding assortment of weapons,
They are everywhere even on transport wagons.
The hooligan has no mercy,
In the morning the streets are messy.

The hooligan displays no conscience;
The hooligan has no human sense;
Some blame it on poverty,
Yet they have affluent property.
They live in a palace like royalty,
 That is where they unleash untold cruelty.

Lord when will this come to an end?
Good God, show the power of your hand.

Let justice get its fulfillment,
Make them stop these killings for entertainment.

The bereaved families lost their beloved sons;
The poor mothers now bear poverty signs;
Fear and sorrow have become their daily bread,
They also wish to see the culprit dead,
It will be a vicious run.

18. A Maniac

Like everyone she carries the sign of the zodiac;
She is a conquering maniac;
She is a patient man-haunter,
She wields the weapons of a game hunter.
She doesn't have time to rest,
In men-hunting game she is the beast.

The maniac smells of attraction,
But hers bears sweet destruction.
Like a fox she is rearing to go;
She parades her beauty at the disco;
Her terrain is the street corner,
In darkness she is a light burner.
Her passion is always boiling,
And garments she is always soiling.

She has mastered the rules of the game,
Those who meet her are never the same.
She carries her heart too light,
Like a network mainframe she has no fight.

She thinks in terms of chinks,
Any hardened heart melts when she winks.

19. Heart's Parlour

We are trapped in our hot and steamy parlour,
Our minds and hearts are in common.
We labour to give our love a true colour;
We swim in the sea of love like salmon;
We never fail to hit the mark,
So do not resist, let us start our lark.

We are in our hearts' parlour,
Let us display our uninhibited valour.
Don't ever keep your passion at bay,
Letting it flow freely will pay.
Don't give my whispering a deaf ear,
Get the message loud and clear.
Don't ever pretend to be blind,
Your heart is the maid of your eyes and mind.

Don't let me down until the break of dawn,
For boredom in our love parlour breeds a yawn.

20. Kajivanah

This is the people's car,
Everyone in here is treated on par.

It fares well at affordable prices;
It comes handy in times of crisis;
Put my heavy luggage on your carrier,
You are really my shining warrior.

Some scorn says you are no good,
You make me laugh when you have no hoot.
Your thundering move clears the road ahead,
Nobody dares to have a sleepy head.
On a muddy day you always slip,
When your bald tyres fail to grip,
You sometimes get unprovoked puncture,
Everyone would freeze at that crucial juncture.

Your speed is unlimited with no speedometer;
Every revving consumes a petrol litre;
You are creaking all the way home,
Warm rooms to relax after a long roam.

21. Shanty Town

It is hell on earth,
Where there is no smile on the young mother,
Yet she has just given birth.
She has one more hunger cry to smother;
Survival is merely on charity;
Handouts will be thrown at her,
While the rich man boosts his smug vanity.

A hard knock in the shanty town,
That is where the poor have settled down.
We lay our hope on the garbage;

Regardless we never lose courage;
We battle against hunger,
Our children don't live longer.

We battle against winter coldness;
We cannot defeat summer wetness;
Politicians give us a good voting soak,
Yet they hide under Samaritan cloak.
Their broad smiles turn into snarls;
Service delivery vehicles become snails,
Goal posts are once again shifted.

22. Lying Eyes

Winking to trap the victim,
Disabling the looker's witty system;
Just like the fisherman throwing the net;
Like a knight throwing down the gauntlet,
You are uneasily sure of victory,
When manipulating your make-believe story.

You plunge in the hook,
Wearing your python look.
Your face is decorated with droopy eyes,
Your catch is the unwise.

You are always restless,
Just like a lone hunter,
You adroitly tear the group asunder.
Those who love to be reckless,
Many have been caught in your web,
Your shore will soon be exposed in the ebb.

23. They Want my Life

They want to wipe me away,
But Almighty keeps them at bay.
They waylay me,
They don't want to let me be.

They are peeled by my positive philosophy;
I resist their myopic ideology,
Then they employ underground methodology.
Hypocrisy is what they master,
When dispatched to kill they work faster.

They want my life,
They cultivate seeds of strife.
They come crawling at night;
Almighty Angels give them a fierce fight,
Like dry leaves they fall.
I crush them underfoot and walk tall,
They become manure while I come of age,
I will forever be under God's tutelage.

24. Political Violence

A gun, a bomb blast and an axe hack,
The people have lost peace track.
It is political violence;
The young are shorn of their innocence;
Through their hands millions of lives are lost,
The nation pays the highest cost.

Many have lost their parents,
Blood flows in torrents,
Soon they will come for you,
That's when you vanish like morning dew.
This fighting makes no sense,
Everybody seems so tense.

They all shift the blame,
To survive one has to veil one's name.

25. Bankruptcy

Bankruptcy, bankruptcy is no good,
One only tastes acrid sweat food.
Without money,
You will never taste love's honey.
In friendship you don't stand a slim chance,
Beauties won't give you a second glance.

Brother you won't taste a good time,
All you will know is a bad rhyme.
Money nowadays decides human dignity,
The loaded think you lost your humanity.
Money imprisons many people,
Black and white turns to purple.

No money, no invitation,
You get no recognition.
People play you like a drum,

You are sometimes labeled a scum.
Invisible, people pass you by without a greeting,
The rich don't hesitate to give you a beating,
What will you do?

26. Classy Hypocrites

Beware, beware of them,
They are classy hypocrites.
They have mastered how to condemn,
They purport to be true democrats.
They have mastered the people's songs,
But they are hell's fork prongs.
Look out for their hidden agenda,
They know how to spread propaganda.

Behold they play a Good Samaritan,
They burn you and blame it on suntan.
They grill you in poverty,
And you are blamed for impurity.
All you have to do is love your brother,
Sister, don't ever bow to the devil's bother.

They speak the people's language,
But they promote carnage.
Why push tribalism,
When it can only obstruct unity?
Why practice sectionalism,
When it only promotes impunity?

27. Drunkard

Why always drink beer?
My brother that is doing you no good;
Your family is living in fear,
And your children forage for food,
Since you have become a dumb drunkard,
You have made your children's lives so hard.

Please give clean life a chance,
Your life comes only once.
Your wife is always in burning tears,
Your children wear neighbour's jeers.
Hot stuff inflames you,
Words out of your mouth are like a loo,
Brother, you have to change.

28. The Loose

You think you own the earth,
You are a risk to people's health.
You walk with your nose in the air,
But you have become a funfair;
A playground you are to all and sundry.

Remember you are just like a flower,
In its bloom it has attraction power.
It attracts insects of all kinds,
They suck without applying their minds.
Your honey is found with ease,

Yet it carries an incurable disease.

Your throne is in the world of fantasy,
There you thrive like crazy.
You detest the word clean;
In the filth you plant your bean;
That is where it thrives,
In grime the ungodly survives.

29. The Pond

When problems abound,
You don't have to run to the pond.
Whenever you meet a puzzle,
You don't have to choose a muzzle.
Patience could be a solution,
Whenever you are overloaded with emotion

Engage your cool head,
Do not rush to disturb the herd.
There cannot be a short-cut;
If you want to get out of the rut,
So my brother be a man,
And you my sister can be a real woman.

Do not be a rat,
There is no need to whine like a spoilt brat.

30. The Future

The future is waiting,
It is anticipating,
Arms are outstretched,
They are longing for you to be touched.
Don't wait for anybody's grace,
Reach out to your rightful place.

Get a place under the Sun,
You will see it is more fun.
The future is around the corner;
It must not find you still a groaner;
Arise and shine,
Climb cloud nine.

Just below your nose,
There reside mental riches,
Give your torn grit some stitches.
Your conscience is like a hose,
With it you water down your seed bed.

31. Thank You My Lord

You gave me life,
Help me respect human life.
Lord of righteousness,
Wipe away selfishness.
I pray that You keep the righteous alive,
Your Mighty Hand should make the weak survive.

You gave me ears,

Help me listen to Your Word through the years.
Almighty God You gave me eyes,
Help me see the truth and become wise.

Lord You gave me a mouth and a voice,
Let me bellow out a just revolutionary noise,
Let me scare the wild birds from my corn,
Let me not make children a scorn.

Lord You gave me hands;
Let them not pillage the innocent's lands;
Let them not harm the harmless creature,
That is the beauty of nature.

32. The Crown

Give Jimmy his crown,
He is now fully grown up and brown.
Why do you prune a shady tree?
It has grown and everyone likes its shade;
It is evergreen and in good shape,
Do not make the resting birds flee.

For years you have pretended deafness;
For ages you have faked blindness;
You are panicking so you muffle every critic,
You have long been living like a tick.
You have created puppets,
And you ignore the words of the prophets.

How sweet it will be,

When you hand it over with a smile,
So that the pinned down will be free.
An intelligent man's mind is like a file,
The history of reality is found in its drawers.

33. What Love Can Do

Love is sweeter than honey,
Facing your crush makes your stomach runny.
Love is as refreshing as water in a fountain;
But when it becomes difficult to contain;
Before your eyes it dries,
You begin to hear agonising cries.

Love makes you hopeful,
You naively never become doubtful.
You never see the blindfolding wool,
It can also make you a dope fool.
When you become achingly restless,
Love can make you careless.
It can make you feel inside out,
Yes, it can drive you away from the crowd.

Love can make you fail to sleep,
You wonder if your gem you can keep,
You become jittery,
You wonder why the loved one is so slippery.

Love can make you sad;
It can drive you mad;
And when you are out of your head,

All you do is twist in your bed.

34. My Father

You have shown the love of a true father;
When others' love reached their short-lived limit;
Yours could easily proceed further,
To my well-being you never failed to commit.

You often took me out of the lion's jaws;
Your love for me is without flaws;
When thunderstorms and tornadoes threatened me,
You provided an unshaken fortress.
You broke the chains of misery to set me free,
Your orders chastened me when I would digress.

Your stern hands fortified my stance like rock pillars;
You soothed the burns of my haters' grillers;
Your fiery praise eroded my timidity,
Your humbleness cultivated the seeds of humility,
I will forever love you, Daddy.

35. Miss Marvel

I was on my daily tiring travel,
En route my eyes got arrested,
My brain was chained by merry Miss Marvel.
I decided to have her tested,
Then I reached out to touch,
She would be a real mouthwatering catch.

But lo, she knew the song I couldn't sing,
She wouldn't dance to mine.
I went to church for a blessing,
So that she would read my hand sign.
She was more eye-catching than a marble,
Her lips were more tantalizing than an apple.

All I could say was a mumble;
She had depleted my words reservoir,
I couldn't help it but make a silly fumble.
My wooing department became void,
All workers had gone on strike.
That speech-impaired damsel,
She is the one I will always like,
Lord knows I have no lies to sell.

36. The Mercenary

The enemies buy you to terminate our brothers,
You bring tears in the eyes of hapless mothers.
Why do you quench the oppressor's blood thirst?
You crucify our heroes,
Just like it was done to Jesus Christ.
Your so-called rebel is the poor people's hero,
In your heart compassion is minus zero.

You diligently serve in the wrong infantry,
Guns and bombs fill up your pantry.
The whole neighbourhood has gone amok,

Peace and justice have gone up in smoke.
Oppressor bosses have gone crazy,
That is the reason why they know no mercy.

There is a bullet in a martyr's brain,
To the masses you heartlessly inflict pain.
You are the one wont to pull the happy trigger;
Everyday your trail of blood grows bigger,
With you around the roads ahead are hazy.

37. Don't Wake Me Up

Don't wake me up as I am having a sweet dream;
In my dream arch enemies are working as a team;
The whole world is full of joy,
There is no weapon built to destroy.

In this world there is no racial prejudice;
There is no backbiting malice;
Hardcore bigots are cleansed of stereotype,
Everybody is smoking a peace pipe.

There is trust between usual predator and prey,
Children of all colours are coming together to play.
The ailing people are healed of their diseases,
Laughter in the air increases.

There is no bomb,
There is no tomb.

38. Whose Scars are These?

With pen and paper they drew,
The misguided thought they knew,
They called their end product boundaries.
They gave themselves territories,
Now you need a passport to pass.
I call them scars;
Brothers were torn from their brothers,
Sisters were cut from their sisters.
At the border the guards are stationed to watch;
With guns and knives they stop our long march,
Alien seeds were sown now we reap xenophobia,
Stooges are living in fleeting utopia.

Your promised freedom has faded like foam,
Now give me back my freedom to roam!

39. The Vote

Many are called on to vote,
It is the swaying right politicians love to erode.
Naivety and blind loyalty make their fertile soil;
Like a rearing snake they coil;
Waiting to bite those who threaten their terrain,
Puppet guards they love to train.

Those who become the bastions of their pillage;
Like ploughs they run rough shot in village tillage,
The loyal bury the seeds in the soil for the boss,
The crops will be reaped with a voting cross.

Elections time babies are kissed for the camera,
All of a sudden it is a compassion era.
The hands of nonentities are shaken with a smile,
When elections are over life reverts to bile.

40. Transparency

Hands are locked together for the public,
It's all gleams on the faces at a picnic.
Behind the scenes,
Hands are clasped into knockout fists;
Frowns have conquered smiles at feasts;
Rooms have turned into realms of dark things,
Doves are nursing broken wings.

Why hug and kiss for public misinformation?
Behind the scenes, we have a different intonation;
We cook plots and ploys;
We hire henchmen as decoys,
All these are done to augment our ego,
We tread on the red carpet wherever we go.
It is all or nothing for our insatiable greed;
We give a blind eye to society's need,
Like ostriches we bury our head in the sand,
We pronounce death to the opposing brand.

So many things behind the scenes,
They are so hideous to even shame sins.
Yes they remain in the dark corner,
That is where you can find the rebel banner.

We need transparency,
Treat it as a matter of urgency.

41. Full Of Love

I am full of love,
I am guilty as charged,
You can put me in handcuffs.
My feelings of affection will always be discharged;
This feeling, no amount of repression will quell,
In my eyes your beauty has no equal.

Friends say I am putty in your hands,
I am glad every one of them understands,
You are the only one who brings a smile to my face.
I have power of attorney to utter my case;
I am in love with you,
Pursuing you is all I'll ever do.

I don't want people thinking I'm a stalker,
Say yes as you know I'm no smooth talker.

42. Pretty Lady

Pretty Lady, I love calling a spate a spate,
Shall we go out on a date?
Please tell me when you'll be available,
Tell me, is your love attainable?
Tell me, what does it take?

I'll do whatever, as I know what is at stake.

I would love to take you out,
Let's join the merry making crowd.
We'll be lost in the groove;
I'll teach you the move;
It will be a piece of cake,
I won't give you a break.

I know of good places,
Where we'll meet happy faces,
Where people are having fun,
Where there is no gun;
There is tied security at the door,
People are swinging and gyrating on the floor.

43. The Convicted

You killed the innocent in cold blood;
You caused blood of the masses to run like flood,
Crimes against humanity you committed.
Now that you are defeated and convicted,
Won't you say an eye for an eye is worth a try?
Don't you think it would be fair?
You also have made others cry.

Like a predator many throats you have slit;
Their bodies and dreams you threw down the pit;
In their bodies thousands of bullets you buried,
You successfully made their deaths hurried.
Now with tears in your eyes you look up the sky;
You are saying a prayer to The Most High,

You are shamelessly begging for mercy.

Do you really have sense of justice?
Their bodies you didn't leave in one piece.
You blame it on poverty,
You blame it on the name of a party,
You plead for a mere whip,
That can only make you briefly weep.
Remember you made others forever mourn;
You even deprived them of their corn,
Why?

44. The Torch

With your dexterous touch,
You gave us a burning torch.
With its light we chase away darkness;
With your wisdom we defeat wickedness;
You are head and shoulders above the rest,
In our hearts you will always be the best.

You have taught us how to conquer adversity;
You showed us how to perform generosity,
The whole wide world sings your name.
You have shown all how well to play the game;
Through your teachings we know justice,
Your words are the bastion of peace.

You'll forever dwell in living memory,
We'll keep on praising God for His glory.

45. The Corrupt

Corruption polluted you to the bone;
You are sucking everybody into your cyclone;
Yes, you are corrupt to the marrow,
Your bliss is the poor people's sorrow.
Your naïve lies undermine our intelligence,
You master the spinning game like science.

You are sitting on our back,
Like a caravan you make us carry your loot sack.
Ironically you still claim to have our interest,
Our genuine concerns are turned into a jest.
You display your mountain of arrogance,
Then you flaunt your loot with a smug prance.

The words rights and freedom make you cross;
You ensure that your heavy lead makes you the boss;
We pant under your weight,
Our cringing and wailing make you feel great.
The poor fall for your cheating,
The witty get a beating.
The poor part with their sweat drenched money,
Our bitter agony is your sweet honey.

Many still cannot see through your plain pretense,
Their blind trust still becomes intense,
That is why the righteous always pray,
You should also have your day.

The End

www.ingramcontent.com/pod-product-compliance
Lightning Source LLC
Chambersburg PA
CBHW060644030426
42337CB00018B/3439